I0345681

THIS BOOK BELONGS TO

_____

A NOTE TO PARENTS

This book on Obedience is part of the Really Cool series. Obedience is a very vital trait children should know, understand, embrace and live by. The Bible says: "Some people are still stubborn after they have been corrected many times. But they will suddenly be hurt beyond cure." Proverbs 29:1 (ICB)

The importance of obedience can not be overemphasised, hence the need for this children's book. It points out to them that there are rewards for obeying their parents and consequences for disobedience.

As parents we have been given the mandate to train our children in the ways of the Lord, as Proverbs 22:6 reminds us. This can be narrowed down to one thing – "Obedience to God".

Key Focus: Obedience to God, Parents, and Authorities.

Obedience is Really Cool

by
Lauretta Amata Olowu

Sam's parents taught him and his sister, Sarah about obedience. They read the bible to them from the book of Ephesians chapter six verses one, two and three and explained the reward for obedience and the outcome of disobedience.

Sam was excited about the rewards of obedience. On his bed he spent some time reading what his parents taught him from the bible.

The next morning he decided to tidy up his room just as his mum had told him to do. While he was tiding up, his friend James came to visit.

"Hello Sam, looks like you're busy. Stop that and let's go to Adam's birthday party," said James excitedly.

"Oh! I'd love to, but Mum said I can't." Sam replied.

"Why?" asked James in shock.

"Wait a minute Sam, are you saying you are not going because your Mum told you so?" James asked.

"My Mum said I shouldn't go but am going anyway, so why can't you?" James said.

"Because I have to obey my Mum and beside am tiding up my room," replied Sam.

"Obedience is cool," Sam added.

"My Mum said she doesn't like the way Adam's friend, Callum, plays with other children," said Sam.

"It doesn't matter what your Mum says, everyone knows Callum is very naughty. Let's go," James replied.

"No, I can't. I have to obey my Mum. Yesterday Mum read the bible to me and made me understand the reward for obedience and the outcome of disobedience to parents," Sam told James.

"What is the reward for obedience?" James asked.

"When I obey my parents, everything will be fine with me and I will have favour with God and my parents. Obeying my parents will also prevent me from being hurt," Sam replied.

"Really," said James.

"Yes James," Sam replied.

"Emm… what about disobedience?" asked James.

"You will be exposed to dangers and lack of blessings from God and your parents." Sam answered.

"I'll take the chance," said James.

"You are missing real fun, I'm going. Bye Sam," said James.

"Bye James, be very careful," Sam said sadly.

James rode to Adam's house, which was at the next building.

"I'm going to have lots of fun. Besides, it's just the next building, so it's ok if I disobey Mum," said James, as he tried to convince himself that it was alright to disobey his Mum (since it was just the next building).

At Sam's house, Sam's Dad was washing his car, Sam came to help him.

"Dad, I told James I can't go to Adam's party because Mum said I shouldn't and he said I'm missing out on having fun." Sam said.

"Don't worry son, soon you will understand that obedience is good," Dad told Sam with a smile.

"I want you to know that I am very proud of you son," said Dad.

"Thank you Dad!" Sam replied.

In the kitchen, Sarah was excited to help her Mum after understanding the rewards of obedience.

"Mum, I will never disobey you because obedience is cool," said Sarah.

"That's lovely," Mum replied.

"I am proud of you Sarah," Said Mum.

"Thank you Mum," Sarah said.

At the party, while everyone was playing, Adam's friend Callum stood behind James and pushed him.

Charlotte barely escaped but James was unlucky as he hit his knee on the edge of the bouncer and got himself injured.

"Oh no," James screamed. "I'm hurt, I should have listened to Mum. Callum is very naughty," said James with tears rolling down his cheek.

"Sam's Mum was right, Callum is very naughty," cried James.

Sam heard what happened to James and decided to visit him. He found James crying in his room.

"I told you not to go, but you didn't listen," Sam said.

"We can't be too wise not to obey our Parents," said Sam. Pointing to James, Sam said:

"Do you know that the bible in the book of Proverbs chapter three verse seven says, "Don't depend on your own wisdom. Respect the Lord and refuse to do wrong things."

James told Sam that he was really silly to have disobeyed his Mum and now he understands how obeying his parents can keep him from trouble.

With a smile on his face, Sam encouraged James to wipe his tears and sit on the bed.

"Do you also know that the book of Proverbs chapter one verses eight and nine says "My child, listen to your father's teaching. And do not forget your mother's advice. Their teaching will beautify your life. It will be like flowers in your hair or a chain around your neck." Sam said.

"Thank you Sam, now I know that obedience is really cool," Said James.

ACTIVITIES

What does the book of Ephesians chapter six verses one and two say.

....
....

What does obedience mean to you?

....

What lesson do you think James learnt?

....

What is your favourite part in the story and why?

....

Reference bible: Int'l Children's bible (ICB)

PRAYER

Dear children, to live an obedient life, you need Jesus to help you. Say this simple prayer, "Lord Jesus, I believe you are the son of God. I believe you can save me from my sin and help me live an obedient life. I give you my heart, come and be my Lord and my saviour in Jesus name, Amen."

SCRIPTURES ON OBEDIENCE

BOOK	CHAPTER	VERSE
Ephesians	6	1,2
Proverbs	1	8,9
Proverbs	3	7
Proverbs	4	1-4,10
Proverbs	6	20-22